WRITING RESPONSIBLY

THIRD EDITION

LOYOLA UNIVERSITY CHICAGO

GENERAL EDITOR
SHERRIE WELLER

FOUNTAINHEAD
PRESS

Our green initiatives include:

Electronic Products
We deliver products in non-paper form whenever possible. This includes pdf downloadables, flash drives, & CDs.

Electronic Samples
We use Xample, a new electronic sampling system. Instructor samples are sent via a personalized web page that links to pdf downloads.

FSC Certified Printers
All of our printers are certified by the Forest Service Council which promotes environmentally and socially responsible management of the world's forests. This program allows consumer groups, individual consumers, and businesses to work together hand-in-hand to promote responsible use of the world's forests as a renewable and sustainable resource.

Recycled Paper
Most of our products are printed on a minimum of 30% post-consumer waste recycled paper.

Support of Green Causes
When we do print, we donate a portion of our revenue to green causes. Listed below are a few of the organizations that have received donations from Fountainhead Press. We welcome your feedback and suggestions for contributions, as we are always searching for worthy initiatives.
Rainforest 2 Reef
Environmental Working Group

Cover and interior design: Doris Bruey

Books may be purchased for educational purposes.

For information, please call or write:
1-800-586-0330
Fountainhead Press
Southlake, TX. 76092
Web site: www.fountainheadpress.com
Email: customerservice@fountainheadpress.com

ISBN 978-1-68036-102-5
Printed in the United States of America

TABLE OF CONTENTS

WRITING RESPONSIBLY

F. Scott Fitzgerald once quipped that "the test of a first-rate intelligence is the ability to hold two opposed ideas in mind at the same time and still retain the ability to function" (41). As an author, Fitzgerald understood that the ability to navigate contradictory viewpoints – to summarize, analyze, synthesize, and develop arguments about a variety of texts – is an essential part of the manner in which writing asks us to interact with a topic from multiple perspectives. As you enter the first phase of your higher education, you'll need to practice and sharpen those analytical and argumentative writing skills you have already developed and begin to understand their importance in dealing with diverse points of view both in and outside the classroom.

The single most misleading myth about writing is that it is an inherent skill: that some have it, others don't, and while the former pursue a life of novel-writing, letters, and memoirs, the rest of us are left with nothing but text messages and tweets of 140 characters or less. Yes, writing comes more intuitively to some students, but it is also a process with identifiable patterns, elements, and stages. The four genres of writing mentioned above – summary, analysis, synthesis, and researched argument – can all be broken down into manageable steps, and with practice, those steps help to create a better and more persuasive piece of writing. In your high school classes, you no doubt studied summary, analysis, synthesis, and argumentation to some degree, but your college classes (and your life beyond that) will require more complexity and sophistication than have been asked of your writing in the past. A thorough understanding of the writing process will allow you to expand your writing capabilities on multiple fronts – from the topics you discuss to the complexity with which you approach them.

And as the range of your writing increases, so will the breadth of what you study. In college, the definition of the term "text" expands exponentially. In addition to the works of classic literature, poetry, history, and the heavy textbooks you are probably accustomed to, your courses at Loyola University Chicago will ask you to analyze graphic novels, newspaper articles, advertisements, political campaigns, speeches, film, music, art, and research studies in psychology, economics, mathematics, science, and medicine. University courses view nearly any document that conveys information or a position about a topic as having intellectual and sociological value, and college-level writing asks you to adeptly compose and respond to this diverse array of texts.

This writing guide is designed to help you anticipate and navigate the sophistication and diversity of writing you will engage in at Loyola. It is organized around the four forms we have already briefly discussed – summary, analysis, synthesis, and argument – and encourages you to view these elements as foundations upon which you can build and develop the skills you already possess. We view college writing as a contribution to ongoing academic discussions; the topics and texts you will study belong to a long history of conversation and debate among scholars, intellectuals, and professionals, and the writing techniques you hone here will allow you to enter those conversations with confidence and complexity.

SUMMARY

As you probably already know, a summary is a sentence, paragraph, or paper that gives an overview of another text. A summary is significantly shorter than its source text, but it still covers the source text's main ideas. The idea behind a summary is that it allows a reader to understand the point or "gist" of the source text without actually reading it.

According to linguists and educators, summary writing is a sophisticated cognitive task. First of all, it demands that the writer reads and fully understands the source text. Then, it requires the writer to select information based on its importance in the source text, to condense details by incorporating them into more general statements, and to integrate all of the selected, condensed materials into an organized structure. In other words, summary writing is more than just deleting insignificant material from the source text; it transforms the source text's details and ideas into a new, more condensed piece (Hidi and Anderson). Research has also shown that knowing how to summarize is crucial for students. Not only is summary writing a common assignment at all levels of education, but it also improves reading comprehension, content-area learning, and information retention (Maclellan; Hidi and Anderson 473; Yu 116-7).

No doubt you have already written a summary at some point in your schooling, and the situations in which you will need to write a summary will only become more frequent at the university level. Across disciplines, university instructors assign summaries in many ways. In class, they might ask for an "overview" of a reading or the "point" of a particular argument. They might require that you write a summary of a text as an introduction to a paper that **analyzes** that text or **synthesizes** it with another text. Also, summary questions often appear on final exams because they not only effectively test reading comprehension but they also require students to identify and prioritize important ideas within a reading. Furthermore, as you progress to upper-division classes, you will be asked to write **research papers** in which you will want to summarize the work of another scholar in order to use it as evidence. In that case, a summary of another person's research will function as part of your own argument.

THE BASICS OF SUMMARY WRITING

Summaries share certain basic characteristics or *conventions*. Most importantly, a summary re-presents or reproduces the content of a source text. A summary is always written in the writer's own words and is shorter than the source text. The following summary of Malcolm X's "A Homemade Education" was written by student Teyana Morgan and conforms to these conventions of summary writing:

> In Malcolm X's "A Homemade Education," he details how creating a self-educational system while in prison allowed him to gain a love for education and new knowledge. While in prison, he explains how he felt incapable of expressing his thoughts and emotions through writing due to his limited vocabulary. This limitation compelled Malcolm X to begin teaching himself. He tells how after teaching himself how to read and write, he began spending a vast amount of time consumed in his newfound literature. Malcolm X describes how studying mostly history and philosophical readings gave him fresh feelings about the knowledge and action of the black race in America. In closing he tells how his homemade education system was more valuable than if he had chosen or had the fate of being anywhere else. Malcolm X gained a freedom in the captivity of prison through immersing himself in new knowledge.

Notice how this summary of "A Homemade Education" demonstrates some of the key characteristics of a well-written summary. To begin with, it does not include any of the student writer's ideas; it focuses on the material in "A Homemade Education." In addition, it is composed entirely in the writer's own words; none of the phrases or sentence structures is taken from Malcolm X's piece. Also, it is much shorter than the source text; Malcolm X's essay is forty-four paragraphs long whereas the summary is only around 150 words. Note as well that the student's summary is a well-constructed paragraph: it contains a topic sentence—in this case, the paragraph's first sentence—that identifies the main idea of "A Homemade Education" and supporting sentences that cover the source text's main points.

The first step in writing a strong summary is knowing when a summary is being asked for by an assignment. The following are essay prompts from various disciplines that ask for some kind of summary:

- What is Vaida's opinion about the importance of water cluster mediated atmospheric chemistry?

- Give an overview of Hanson's and Mohn's discussion on educational assessment trends.

- Summarize Piaget's stages of cognitive development.

- What is Caroline Bird's argument concerning college education?

When looking for key words or phrases that indicate that a prompt is asking for a summary, look for instructions that somehow ask you to re-state what you read in a source. You might see words like "overview," "point," "identify," or "describe." These words, and words like them, ask you to re-encapsulate, but not interpret or analyze, what is in a source text. When this happens, you should examine the prompt more carefully to see if you are being asked to summarize a source. Be aware, too, that sometimes an instructor will ask for a summary and then ask for an interpretation in the same prompt; summaries are frequently used as introductions to arguments and response essays.

In order to write a strong, efficient summary, you will need to understand your source text hierarchically. In other words, you will need to identify the text's main idea, or the idea that encapsulates all the other ideas in the text. Then, you will need to prioritize the main points that support or explain the main idea, understanding that all of the details in the text can be generalized into these main points. In source texts that are already well structured by the author, this task will be relatively easy. However, not all source texts are well organized; often, you will need to analyze the text and infer the hierarchy of ideas. It might help for you to think of a source text in terms of a tree diagram like the one below. Each level encapsulates the levels that are underneath it.

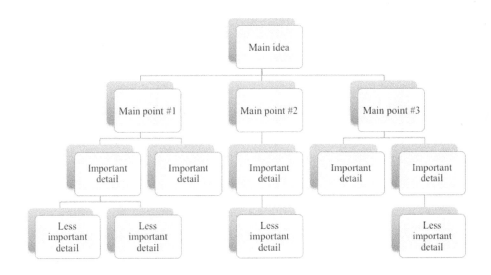

Thinking about a text in this way and ordering information according to importance will help you with many aspects of summary writing. Most · importantly, it will help you to eliminate unnecessary information from your summary, and it will help you group details under more general main points. For example, in the summary above, the writer does not, like Malcolm X, list the books from the prison library that he checked out and read, nor does she tell us exactly what information these books contained. These are details that are generalized in the statement that Malcolm X studied "history and philosophical readings."

Although brevity is a defining feature of a summary, different assignments require different lengths for summaries. Again, thinking of your source text in terms of a tree diagram can help you decide how much information to include in your summary. If you are asked for a single-sentence summary, you will only want to include the first, broadest level of the diagram, the source text's main idea. If you are asked to write a paragraph-length summary (and this is the most common kind of summary), you will probably include only the first two levels of the diagram, the source's main ideas and main points. Although it is rare, you might be asked to summarize a text over several pages; in this case, you might (if there are not too many main points to cover) include the third level of information, some important details.

As you compose your summary, you should be aware that conventions of strong academic writing are still relevant. In other words, your paragraphs should be well organized with a main idea and corresponding topic sentence. Fortunately, your tree chart will provide you with a ready-made structure. For paragraph-length summaries, simply turn the main idea identified in your chart into a topic sentence, and use the main points to fill in the paragraph. If your summary is longer than a single paragraph, decide how to logically divide the main points into several paragraphs, each with its own topic sentence. Usually, you will still state the main idea of the source text at the beginning of the first paragraph.

As we have discussed, a lot of cognitive work goes into writing a strong summary. When students do not fully understand how to write a summary or do not want to do the cognitive work, they often make two crucial mistakes. The first should be obvious from the discussion above: it is the mistake of including too much detail or unimportant information. The second is what is called "patchwriting" or "copy-delete" summarizing. This happens when students copy chunks of the source text, possibly changing some grammar or vocabulary, and stitch these chunks into a single paragraph (Howard 264; Maclellan). Not only does patchwriting fail to accomplish the goals of summarizing, but also, when quotation marks are not used to indicate original phrasing and word choice, it is a form of plagiarism. Below is a summary that exemplifies patchwriting:

> While Malcolm X was in prison, he was jealous of Bimbi and other inmates who could take charge of conversations. He decided to get hold of a dictionary. He copied the first page and read it aloud to himself over and over again. Once his word-base broadened, Malcolm X checked out books from the prison library and joined weekly debates between inmate teams. He loved to read so much that he read at night in his prison cell in the glow from the hallway. Not even Elijah Muhammad could have guessed what a new world opened up to Malcolm X as he learned that the collective white man had acted like the devil by oppressing black people. When people asked Malcolm X where he went to college, he said that prison enabled him to study more than college where there are too many distractions.

If you refer back to Malcolm X's essay, you will see that the writer of this summary has copied much phrasing and vocabulary, not to mention sentence structure, from the source text. In addition, this summary does not generalize details but instead includes an unbalanced sampling of them (with a few misreadings) from different parts of "A Homemade Education." This summary does not show that the writer has understood the source text, processed and prioritized the information in it, and reproduced it in an organized way for her readers.

STRATEGIES FOR WRITING STRONG SUMMARIES

It is important to reflect the source text's genre in your summary. If you don't, your reader will not get a full understanding of your source text. Your job as the summary writer is to give your reader an understanding of not only the content of the source text but also the source text's form – its purpose and structure. For example, if you summarized Malcolm X's essay, which is a narrative, by emphasizing his argument about the "whitening" of history, you would not be giving your readers an accurate idea of what the source text is. "A Homemade Education" tells the story of Malcolm X's education, and it is important that your summary offers a shortened, condensed version of that story, not an analysis of his ideas or an outline of his underlying argument.

Although, in your university classes, you will encounter and be asked to summarize many different kinds of source texts, three of the most common genres you will see are narrative, expository, and argument. These three genres not only have very different structures, but the hierarchies of ideas are different as well. In a source text that is an argument, the main idea is – predictably – the author's thesis or position. Usually, the main points are the author's major reasons that support his or her thesis. Concrete evidence makes up the details that correspond to the author's major reasons. A tree diagram for an argument, then, would look something like this:

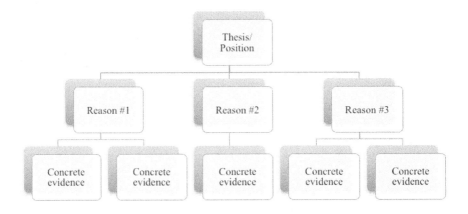

Here, the tree diagram reflects the structure of an argument, which is the source text's genre. A tree diagram for another genre would likely look very different. For example, if we constructed a tree diagram for a narrative, the main idea would not be the thesis of an argument, but a statement of the main action in the narrative. The second level of the diagram, the main points, would be the main plot points in the narrative. On the other hand, an expository text, which is a text that explains something and the purpose of which is to inform the reader, would have as its main idea an overview of the information provided in the source text and more specific statements of fact as the main points. Understanding a source text hierarchically means understanding what kind of hierarchy is in place. That way, your summary will accurately represent the source text's content and form.

At the beginning of this section, you read a summary of a narrative, Malcolm X's "A Homemade Education." Below are a few more examples. Consider, first, this summary of an argument, Caroline Bird's "The Case Against College," which was written by a student in a first-year composition course. As with the other summaries you have read in this section, the first sentence states the main idea of the source text, in this case, the source text's thesis or position, and the following sentences explain the source text's main points, in this case, the argument that supports the thesis:

> Evaluating higher education in "The Case Against College," Caroline Bird questions the effectiveness of such an institution. She argues that the expectations of the value of college may not actually be assessed in college. For example, some expectations people have of what they will derive from college are supposed to be acquired during earlier stages in life. Caroline Bird also discusses how education can be learned elsewhere, such as through books or television, and does not need to be learned in a school setting. Another point that Bird asserts in her argument is that putting the weight of the future of mankind on university students is quite unrealistic. She explains that most students do not know or are too young to have determined their wants for the future. Caroline Bird closes by suggesting that college be closely critiqued by potential students for its possible worth before they make the decision to attend (Morgan).

WRITING RESPONSIBLY

Following the structure of Bird's own argument, this student begins and closes by stating Bird's position. In the middle of the paragraph, she lists some of the main reasons that Bird uses to justify her position.

The next example is a summary written of an expository text, "On the Breeds of Cattle – Historic and Current Classifications." Notice the differences between this summary and those of "A Homemade Education" and "The Case Against College":

> In "On the Breeds of Cattle – Historic and Current Classifica-
> tions," the authors list, sort, and discuss the various systems used
> to classify cattle breeds over the last several hundred years. In
> doing so, they report the difficulties scientists have faced in clas-
> sifying cattle because of the long, largely undocumented history
> of cross-breeding. However, they also detail the reasons why
> classifying cattle is important and why many scientists over the
> years have attempted to establish a classification system. Accord-
> ing to this article, classification systems of the past were based on
> head/horn shape and size, coat color, or geographic origin. More
> modern classification systems have been founded upon modern
> scientific advances; these systems use biochemical traits – often
> in conjunction with previous systems – to classify cattle. The
> most recent developments in cattle classification are DNA-based;
> the article implies that scientists believe that the DNA-based clas-
> sification system is the most accurate and useful.

You can see that, in this summary, the writer focuses on what information is provided by the source text and how that information is presented. The topic sentence, which states the source text's main idea, gives an overview of the information covered in the source. The following sentences break that information down into parts; these sentences discuss exactly how the authors list, sort, and discuss cattle classification systems. Notice that, unlike a summary of an argument, which reproduces the logical framework of an argument, a summary of an expository text reports a set of facts.

Once you have an idea of *what* you want to say in your summary – that is, once you have identified the main idea and main points – you will move on to thinking about *how* you want to say it. There are specific writing strategies, or composition "moves," that effective summary writers use in order to indicate to their readers that the piece they are reading is a summary. Below are some of the common moves summary writers make in their summaries:

- They introduce a written summary by orienting their readers to the author and title of the source text. Here are two different ways of introducing the source text at the beginning of a summary:

  a. "In Malcolm X's 'A Homemade Education,' he tells the story . . ."

  b. "Malcolm X's 'A Homemade Education' tells the story of . . ."

- They refer often to their source as a way of reminding their readers that the information is coming from a source text. Notice below how the writer intentionally refers back to the source text in the phrases, "the narrative" and "Malcolm X":

  a. "The narrative begins by describing his frustration."

  b. "Malcolm X details the many books he encountered in prison."

- They use verbs that are appropriate to the genre of the source text. Below are examples and lists of verbs that correspond to narrative, expository, and argument source texts:

  a. Narrative
    - Example: "Malcolm X *recounts* his experiences learning to read and write."
    - Verbs: *recounts, tells, narrates, describes, remembers*

  b. Expository
    - Example: "The authors *detail* the many classification systems used over the last 100 years."
    - Verbs: *explains, lists, reports, expands upon, details*

  c. Argument
    - Example: "Bird *defends* her position by providing specific examples as evidence."
    - Verbs: *asserts, argues, affirms, reasons, defends, justifies*

To see how these moves work to produce a coherent, clear summary, see the examples provided earlier in this section.

For additional resources on writing summaries, please see *Pearson Writer*. In the *Writer's Guide* tab, search for "Writing Summaries." Also, for tips on using summary in a Summary/Response paper, search the *Writer's Guide* for "How do you write a response paper?"

SAMPLE STUDENT SUMMARY/RESPONSE ESSAY

Annesley Clark

Professor Weller

UCWR 110

9 September 2014

iNeed: A Reflection on Technology Today

People today often find it impossible to fathom living without technology. When an iPhone breaks or the Internet goes down, people of all ages feel anything from annoyance to panic, frustration to rage. In their essays, "A Reunion with Boredom," and "Is Google Making Us Stupid," Charles Simic and Nicholas Carr explore the idea that technology is changing the way people think and live. Both men are suspicious of our clear reliance on technology, and their essays serve as grains of salt to take with our unbending love of electronics. I agree with Carr and Simic that technology is changing the way we live our lives, and that we need to be wary of our dependence on and use of technology.

In "A Reunion with Boredom," Simic explains how his 72 hours without power (and thus, without technology) in the wake of a hurricane allowed him to reflect on how our increased use of technology has changed our lives. He notes that those who are constantly on their phones miss chances to connect with people and surroundings because they are glued to their screens (Simic 374). In the technology-free boredom of Simic's youth, he discovered himself.

He describes coming "face-to-face" with himself and becoming a "spectator of [his] own existence" (Simic 375). Simic used this time with himself to discover who he was and laments that today "we are only puppets jerked this way and that by whatever device we think we are operating" (376). Simic believes that we are losing our uniqueness and our very personalities to our obsession with electronic devices.

While still focused on how we interact with our devices, Carr takes a slightly different approach. In his essay "Is Google Making Us Stupid?" he explores how advances in technology, particularly the advent of the Internet, have changed the way we read and how we think. He first looks at how reading patterns have changed, describing how, ever since he began reading primarily online, his brain "expects to take in information the way the Net distributes it: in a swiftly moving stream of particles" (Carr 92). A scientific study out of the University College London showed that people researching online "power browse" though many different articles, looking at a page or two before "bouncing" to the next article to skim (Carr 93-94). Carr says that when we read in the "power browse" style we've adopted, "Our ability to interpret text... remains largely disengaged" (94). When we read online, we don't process the material the same way we do when we read an actual book.

The Internet is pervasive and powerful. It layers multiple types of media on top of one another, so engaging with only one source of information at a time is rare. The addition of advertisements, games, and accessories also diverts our attention, contributing to our inability to engage with longer texts. Carr goes on to describe Google's agenda and the idea that "The human brain is just an outdated processor that needs a faster processor and a bigger hard drive." (99). The financial backers of the Internet need our brains to function this way – the faster we go, the more money they make off of advertisement, and the more they can learn about their target audience and persuade us to purchase their products and services. (Carr 99-100). After all, Carr recognizes that technological advances have historically been met with opposition. At the same time, however, he is wary of the way the Internet has changed our brains and memories. Carr concludes his powerful essay by reminding the reader about a scene from *2001: A Space Odyssey.* In the world of the film, "People have become so machinelike that the most human character is a machine" (Carr 101). Carr wonders if this is the way we are headed as well.

After taking the time to look at my daily life, I have to agree with both Simic and Carr that constant attachment to our devices has changed us. I can't go an hour without checking my phone, logging on to Facebook, or sending a SnapChat. I absolutely feel addicted to my technology. Most of my social interaction now takes place in the cyber world, and I often find that I would rather text friends than make the effort to see them in person. This scares me, and it should. Seeing my friends should not feel like a chore, but with technology being so easy and readily available, anything that requires more effort seems that much more difficult.

My social life is not the only affected area – my memory and attention span have been impacted as well. Carr describes how the Internet seems to be "chipping away at my capacity for concentration and contemplation," which is an idea I can relate to completely (92). While watching a show online, I often have several other tabs open to check social media, all while playing a game on my phone. I feel that I no longer have the capacity to dedicate all of my attention to one incoming channel, except when settling down to read. When I am sucked into a good book, the world around me blurs. Nothing is more real than what is contained in the pages of my reading. That, in my opinion, is powerful. If none of these new technologies can captivate me the same way a book can, then I need to explore whether they are truly as helpful and important as I think. Luckily, I haven't lost my passion for reading. I try to read at least one non-required book per week, and I still get a rush from reading a great novel, a fascinating memoir, or interesting nonfiction. I don't think I will ever lose my love of books.

At the same time, however, I notice that my ability to read for long spans of time has gone down. Just a few years ago I was reading at least 2-3 books a week. I could curl up in a chair and devour a book in hours. Today this is rare for me because reading requires physical and mental attention. In order to reap the benefits of reading, I have to hold the book, turn the pages, and keep my eyes on the text. With television, the Internet, social media, or Netflix, I can go back and forth between multiple different things at once, providing so many different sources of incoming stimulation that I don't truly have to pay attention to any one of them to feel occupied or to escape boredom.

Simic's and Carr's essays provide an important warning– we need to slow down and carefully examine our relationship with technology. We rarely have time to get to know ourselves, because any "down time" we come across makes us uncomfortable. Even one moment without incoming information makes us nervous – we pull out our phones or turn on some music to take the discomfort of doing nothing away. And the brain-changing style of the Internet has reached incredibly far, even hitting those of us who, like me, consider ourselves avid readers. Even though I love to read, at this point I'm so trained to multitask and synthesize data coming in from all angles that to narrow it down to just words on a page can feel boring. My younger self, the middle school Annesley whose favorite activity was browsing the library and who only asked for books for Christmas, would be appalled to hear that. I can only assume, as Carr and Simic do, that the prevalence of the Internet and Google has changed my brain, and possibly made me a little more stupid.

Works Cited

Carr, Nicholas. "Is Google Making Us Stupid?" *50 Essays: A Portable Anthology*. Ed. Samuel S. Cohen. 4th ed. Boston: Bedford/St. Martin's, 2014. 91-102. Print.

Simic, Charles. "A Reunion with Boredom." *50 Essays: A Portable Anthology*. Ed. Samuel S. Cohen. 4th ed. Boston: Bedford/St. Martin's, 2007. 374-77. Print.

OTHER KINDS OF SUMMARIES

Before concluding, there are a few variations on the standard form of summary, which you should know about. The first is the directed summary,
which is a summary of a particular aspect of a text rather than the whole text
(Strahan, Moore, and Heumann 19-20). So, for example, in a literature class,
you might be asked to summarize Jay Gatbsy's long romance with Daisy
Buchanan in *The Great Gatsby* instead of summarizing the entire novel. Or,
on a psychology exam, you might be asked to summarize the censoring function of the conscious mind rather than the entire text of Freud's *Interpretation
of Dreams*. A directed summary is written just like a standard summary, but
the hierarchy of main ideas and main points is more specific. This is why it is
important to carefully read the prompt or question before you begin writing
your summary.

Another variation on the standard form of summary is the annotated bibliography entry. Typically, an annotated bibliography is formatted like
a normal bibliography, but it also includes a brief summary-like entry,
or annotation, after each source's information. Below is an excerpt from an
annotated bibliography:

> Bird, Caroline. "The Case Against College." *Writing Responsibly:
> Communities in Conversation*. Southlake, TX: Fountainhead
> Press, 2012. 80-84. Print.

> In "The Case Against College," Caroline Bird argues that poten-
> tial college students should consider options other than attending
> college. She provides many reasons that suggest that college has
> been overvalued in American culture. While Bird's argument is
> compelling, much of her evidence is anecdotal and undermines
> the strength of her position. However, the essay is helpful in that
> it gathers many of the most reasonable arguments offered against
> attending college. For my paper, which is an academic essay on
> why attending college is the best option for high school seniors,
> I can use Bird's essay when constructing my counterarguments.

What you include in an annotation always depends on what your instructor asks for. However, usually, the annotation includes at least one, but sometimes all three, of the following elements:

1. A one- to two-sentence summary of the source text;

2. An evaluation of the credibility or general usefulness of the source text and/or how it compares to other sources on the list; and/or,

3. A reflection on the source as to its relevance to or usefulness for your specific project (Bisignani and Brizee).

While, technically speaking, an annotated bibliography entry is not a summary, it almost always includes a summary of the source text. As you can see in the example above, the annotation opens with a summary of Caroline Bird's essay and then continues on to evaluate it and reflect on its usefulness.

For additional resources on annotated bibliographies, please see *Pearson Writer*. In the *Writer's Guide* tab, search for "Writing an Annotated Bibliography."

SAMPLE STUDENT ANNOTATED BIBLIOGRAPHY

Emily Wagner

UCWR 110

23 March 2014

Annotated Bibliography

"Abuse By Men 'Not Considered A Crime' In Many Countries." *Women's Inter-*

national Network News 25.4 (1999): 37. *Academic Search Complete.*

Web. 22 Mar. 2014.

This source is an informative article written for a scholarly journal. The intended audience is activists and scholars interested in human rights, specifically gender-based violence, and the bias is towards the prevention of such crimes, given the nature of the statistics reported. The content of the source features statistics of the number of women and girls subjected to domestic and sexual violence in a number of countries worldwide, as well as outlines the negative impact of such crimes. This source is valuable to me because it helps place a devastating number on the injustices experienced globally by women. It will be useful in constructing my argument because the shocking figures featured in the article will help provide the pathos needed to persuade my audience that violence against women is truly a global issue that needs to be eradicated.

Half the Sky: Turning Oppression into Opportunity for Women Worldwide. Dir.

Maro Chermayeff. Independent Lens, 2012. Film.

This source is an educational documentary. The intended audience is the general public because it aired on PBS, a public TV channel, as well as human right's activists due to the content and charity work demonstrated in the film. It is clearly biased towards helping women become equals in their respective cultures. The source features the stories of women and girls in ten developing countries, their experience with violence and discrimination, and their efforts to fight injustice through education and activism. This source is valuable to me because it provides real-life examples of women fighting their oppression, preventative measures to stop the violence, and benefits of eliminating it. I plan on using this source as an appeal to logic; it will be used to back up my thesis with hard evidence of what good can be done in the world when violence against women is prevented or decreased.

UN Women. United Nations, 2011. Website. 22 March 2014.

This source is a website run by the United Nations, a leader in protecting human rights that provides information about gender based violence in the world and what the UN is doing to stop it. The intended audience is anyone curious about activism and the oppression women face around the world. The site is biased towards women, and helping other countries form legislation and other policies in order to prevent gender-based violence and oppression. This source is valuable to me because it gives great background information on the injustices against women globally, and outlines many of the procedures that are being implemented by other countries and activist groups in order to stop the injustice. I plan on using this source to discuss the techniques used to raise women's status, as well as to provide context for the rest of my argument.

Elakkary, Sally, et al. "Honor Crimes: Review And Proposed Definition." *Foren-*

sic Science, Medicine & Pathology 10.1 (2014): 76-82. *Academic*

Search Complete. Web. 22 Mar. 2014.

This source is an essay written for an academic journal. The intended audience is legislators looking for information on "honor crimes" and how to redefine the term. The bias is towards persecuting those who kill in the name of "family honor." The content of the source features a review of honor crimes, who engages in such acts, the role they play in patriarchal societies, and the reasoning behind their existence. It also discusses the low conviction rate in honor killings and ways to prevent femicide in the name of honor. This source is valuable to me because not only does it outline in detail the motives behind honor killings and an accepted definition, but it also recommends some solutions in stopping this violence. I plan on using the source to describe one out of the many facets of gender-based violence, as well as support the claim that there are solutions to the problems women face.

Sharma, Monica. "Twenty-First Century Pink Or Blue: How Sex Selection Tech-

nology Facilitates Gendercide And What We Can Do About It." *Family*

Court Review 46.1 (2008): 198-215. *Academic Search Complete.* Web.

22 Mar. 2014.

This source is an essay written for an academic journal. The intended audience is those who are concerned with the family court system, including judges, attorneys, mediators and professionals in mental health and human services. The bias is against sex selection in the cases of gendercide. The source contains a description of different sex selection technologies, and how in cultures where boys are valued higher they are being abused in order for families to have male children. It also discusses many of the negative implications of gendercide and female infanticide, as well as the cultural ideologies behind this phenomenon. This source is valuable to me because it directly discusses the negative impacts in the world relating to gendercide and what is being done to stop it. I plan on using this source as an appeal to logic; it gives hard evidence and facts in order to prove to the reader that the world will benefit when gender-based violence is stopped.

Smith, Christine, Rebecca Paulstone and Sarah Kahando. "A Model of Wom-

en's Educational Factors Related to Delaying Girls' Marriage." *Inter-*

national Review of Education 58.4 (2012): 533-555. *Academic Search*

Complete. Web. 22 Mar. 2014.

This source is an essay written for an academic journal. The intended audience is those who are interested in scholarly information on major educational innovations, research projects, and trends. The bias is towards educating girls and women in order to prevent them from marrying so young. This source contains a review of all of the problems associated both economically and socially with early marriage and a description of what factors can prevent marriage. It also outlines many of the benefits of educating young women and girls. This source is valuable to me because it clearly discusses many of the benefits of preventing girls from marrying so young, which directly supports my argument that stopping crimes against women can only benefit society.

Ulltveit-Moe, Tracy. *Lives Blown Apart: Crimes against Women in Times of*

Conflict, Stop Violence against Women. London: Amnesty International, International Secretariat, 2004. Print.

This source is a non-fiction book printed by Amnesty International, a leader in protecting human rights. The intended audience is those who are interested in the role of women in wartime and what is being done to prevent the serious breach of human rights in times of violence. The bias is towards preventing gender-based violence used in wartime and encouraging peaceful measures instead. This source contains many first-hand accounts of survivors of armed conflicts, an analysis of a woman's role in war, both as a civilian and a soldier, and numerous recommendations on how to prevent gender-based violence as an act of war. This source is valuable to me to me because it provides copious amounts of first hand experiences and anecdotes, which can be used as an appeal to emotion in my argument in order to persuade the reader that gender-based violence is a human rights violation and not just an act of war.

ANALYSIS

Simply put, analysis is a detailed examination and investigation of the elements of a text, often a piece of writing, literature, art, film, or music. As students, you engage in analysis in nearly every facet of your daily academic lives: in classroom discussions about economic policy, literary theory, or history; in biology labs; in law practicums or in pre-med study groups. Analysis occurs in the form of engaged study, discussion, and dissection that leads to a deep understanding of a subject and its importance, effects, and implications for the future.

In the previous section, we discussed how an effective **summary** condenses a text to its core elements and arguments and re-presents them in a way that is concise and clear. While summarizing, writers need to search for the main points that comprise a text and then separate important details that support these core points from the other secondary elements in the text. In a way, the process of summarizing a text involves analysis; determining the main arguments of a text and prioritizing the evidence and detail that an author gives in support of these points requires a writer to think critically about which elements are most important to a novel, film, essay, or work of art. More than a rote memorization of facts, analysis is the ability to critically evaluate a work and come to a conclusion about it.

As we've said, analysis is a central part of a student's academic work, and it is a requirement in essays, discussions, and assignments in most (if not all) classes you will take in college. It is also important to grasp that analysis can be applied to any imaginable text. You are probably accustomed to being asked to analyze written stories in your high school English classes, but consider how in film studies courses students analyze the themes, lighting, plot, shot construction, cinematography, and dozens of other components of a movie. In history courses, professors ask students to evaluate the factors that lead to and surround an event and perhaps to analyze the outcomes or the solutions proposed by historical figures. In nursing and pre-med courses, the patients are the texts, and the students determine the best course of treatment using facts or inferences gleaned from a patient's condition and the student's own knowledge of medical treatment. Advertisements, cartoons, news stories, business meetings, works of music, or political speeches are all texts that you can analyze.

While analysis relies on some of the same skills that you use when summarizing, remember that analysis extends beyond summarization. Good analysis implicitly *makes an argument* about the text – for example, its subject matter, its format, its rhetorical strategies, its origin – and so the most effective analyses do not simply restate what the original text says. A compelling piece of analysis examines specific elements of a text and then evaluates them for meaning or effectiveness. The following example of analysis is a paragraph drawn from an actual student's response to Alan Moore's graphic novel *Watchmen*. In it, this student analyzes the nature of the character Rorschach:

> The character Rorschach elicits varied, yet strong, responses from readers. Throughout the novel, Rorschach reacts to events with an absolute, black-and-white manner. He is guided by a conservative, fundamental set of morals from which he never wavers. For example, when Rorschach and Nite Owl II learn about Veidt's scheme, and the deceit and murder involved, Rorschach reacts by saying, "No. Not even in the face of Armageddon. Never Compromise" (20). Although Veidt argues he is acting for the greater good, Rorschach cannot see past the use of Veidt's amoral means to an end. This scene in particular is an instance where the reader identifies with Rorschach; we are just as surprised and disgusted at the turn of events as he is, and therefore, we identify with him. Rorschach is perhaps attractive to the reader because he is a concrete viewpoint in a story where right and wrong are hazy.

This student's analysis is effective for a number of reasons. To start, the student begins with a claim about the role of the character Rorschach in *Watchmen*, suggesting that he is an uncompromising character with a clear moral code (that he "reacts to events with an absolute, black-and-white manner").

Then, the student supports that claim with a quote from the text as evidence of how Rorschach responds to a complex situation with unwavering certainty. The last portion of the paragraph is the most significant; in it, the student contends that the Rorschach character, despite holding some extreme views, is nonetheless appealing to the reader because his "concrete viewpoint" represents moral certitude in a story where good and bad always seem to be in flux. This student's analysis is stylish and perceptive and attempts to draw larger conclusions about the text from the smaller element being analyzed in this particular paragraph.

APPROACHING ANALYSIS ASSIGNMENTS

Instructors approach analysis in a variety of ways. While many will ask you to analyze the work and ideas of others, you also will be asked to turn the lens of analysis back on yourself and your own work. In the following sample assignment, drawn from an actual course, the instructor asks students to analyze the impact of their disciplinary background on a difficult or controversial issue.

> **Assignment:** This project asks you to analyze an issue of public importance from the context of your disciplinary background or interests. The project will have two parts, detailed below:
>
> You will choose a single issue of public significance and produce an analysis of the issue, its current stakes, and its importance or future implications. For example, you might explore how the current public debate about the balance between government spending and the need to reduce the deficits affects public employees in Chicago. Or, you might examine issues of environmental awareness, public health, or union funding. Whichever issue you choose, you need to analyze its parameters, stakes, and implications.
>
> You will then turn to an analysis of your topic from the perspective of your disciplinary field (if you have not declared a major, simply pick a subject area that you might like to study in the future). What does your field of study/interest have to contribute to the larger public debate about the issue? Are there specific concerns for your field in regards to this topic? Are there certain elements, theories, or practices from your field that will help illuminate the issue or more effectively work toward a solution?

Through the assignment, the instructor is encouraging students to draw numerous connections between their class and a real-world issue and between that issue and their disciplinary background. Requiring a disciplinary reflection means the student must analyze their own work and begin to think critically about the ways in which their individual studies will intersect with the world outside the classroom. Below is a brief excerpt from a student response to this assignment:

> The English discipline plays a huge role in the issue of immigration and immigration laws, not only when it comes to the immigrants and aspiring US citizens, but the people who are trying to change and rectify this issue through rhetoric, argumentation, and persuasion. These are all skills learned in the English discipline and can be used when trying to sway a certain group a certain way. Many news stations such as FOX News and MSNBC constantly talk about the issue of immigration and what it means to this country, but both networks have very different viewpoints when it comes to this issue.

This student is attempting to connect the discipline of English to the issue of immigration reform. In this paragraph, she notes that English is important not only because literacy and language fluency is a central component of the immigration debate, but also because the skills that English students practice are needed to navigate the public debate over immigration reform. Processing the arguments made in different outlets – from FoxNews, MSNBC, and many places elsewhere – and determining their persuasiveness requires critical thinking. In essence, she is suggesting that navigating a public debate demands analysis skills. In connecting the skills of English majors to a contemporary public controversy, this student uses the same skills of analysis that she suggests the discipline of English provides.

A METHODOLOGY FOR ANALYSIS
Though there are many ways to approach analysis – and we encourage you to develop your own, specific to your preferences, the context of your writing, and your discipline – here are a few critical steps to get started with analysis:

1. **Begin with the text.** Strong analysis begins by being exceptionally familiar with the text. You can't analyze a text successfully unless you have identified its main points and clarified for yourself any moments of confusion. For example, are there any vocabulary terms

that you do not understand? Look them up. Are there any references to outside events and information that you do not know – for example, historical figures or movements? Again, research these things until you are comfortable with the ins-and-outs of the text. Not only will this research make you more familiar with the text, it will give you more insightful things to say in your analysis and ensure your credibility as an informed authority on the topic.

2. **Start small.** Because analysis requires that you define and defend an arguable claim, the best way to find this claim is by using the text(s). Think of yourself as a lawyer in a courtroom, and the text is your best and most persuasive piece of evidence! Identify the pieces of the text(s) you are interested in and then ask yourself these questions: What do these things tell me? What is the effect these pieces of evidence have on the text overall, or in comparison to other texts, or on how I understand the subject matter? Are there any pieces of evidence available that contradict each other or my assumptions?

Notice that we are advocating that you start with your evidence and only then build a claim. You are more likely to achieve a defendable claim when you *work from* the text than if you *look for* specific moments to defend a pre-existing assumption. Why? Because you end up plundering the text for only those facts or moments that support your idea, which makes it easy to overlook evidence that doesn't fit or may even overrule your claim.

3. **Define your claim.** Analytical claims can be as big as the whole thesis for a dissertation or as small as a simple, conversational declarative sentence like, "Brian Urlacher is the most consistent middle linebacker in the NFL." Regardless of whether they require ten pages or ten seconds to defend, claims need to be **specific**. Spend time identifying just what you want to argue and how. In the same way that summary requires that you to make clear all the parameters of another person's argument, analysis requires that you make clear all the parameters of your own argument.

Be incredibly intentional with your word choice; generalizations always hurt an argument and make it harder for your reader to anticipate the steps you will take to defend your claim. For example, in the statement made above, it matters whether the writer argues that Brian Urlacher is the *best* middle linebacker or the *most consistent*. A reader can anticipate how the writer will defend the claim that Urlacher is the "most consistent" middle linebacker by using statistics and comparisons with other middle linebackers in the NFL. It would be much harder to anticipate, and to argue, that he is simply the "best" without relying too much on opinion. If you are thoughtful about the words you choose to define your claim, it should provide you with a blueprint for the rest of your analysis.

4. **Quote, summarize, and paraphrase selectively to guide your interpretation.** As we mentioned above, the text is your best piece of evidence. Use it carefully and constructively to advance your claim. Remember, though, that evidence – particularly quotations – don't speak for themselves; your analysis should indicate *how* you want your reader to understand the textual evidence. It is your responsibility as a writer to drive the conversation with your insights. Phrases such as "this demonstrates," "which results in," or "revealing that" can provide helpful clues to your reader and will force you to make strong choices about how the evidence should be interpreted.

5. **Work outward.** The most effective pieces of analysis consider a range of implications beyond the specific text being analyzed. It's not enough to simply make a claim when analyzing for the sake of making a claim; your audience should understand why your claim matters, and you should be able to answer the age-old question, "So what?" There are a number of different ways to work outward when analyzing. In the immigration and disciplinary reflection example we looked at before, the student considers the impact of the field of English on the public debate over immigration. While her narrow conclusion is that the skills of analysis taught in an English classroom will help a person navigate the contentious arguments related to immigration reform, her work also implies that those analytical skills can serve a person in processing nearly any controversial public debate. Your analysis does not necessarily need to be connected to national or international issues like immigration reform, but working outward from the text can be valuable.

Once you have made an argument about a text, consider how your con-clusions relate to other texts you have read or watched. Are there paral-lels or differences? You should also consider the larger themes or discus-sions that you have studied in your course. Does this particular text have something new or significant to say about a topic of interest to your class? Does it bring you any closer to fully understanding a subject? Knowledge is found in the fissures and overlaps of ideas, and you can illuminate yourself (and your fellow students and instructor) as to how the thoughts and arguments in one text relate to the bigger picture.

Consider the following example of student work as a model of the meth-odology we proposed. The student was asked to write a brief analysis of a play, Henrik Ibsen's *The Wild Duck*, specifically examining its themes of ill-ness and blindness:

> Ibsen's *The Wild Duck* connects Gregers's inability to understand what is really happening within himself to blindness and physi-cal sickness. Gregers is driven by guilt from not helping his friend Hjalmar Ekdal's family at a critical time in the past. By revealing the lies within Hjalmar's marriage, Gregers convinces himself that he has saved his friend from living a life that is not his own. However, his help actually is very poisonous to the Ekdal fam-ily, because Gregers himself, according to the doctor Relling, is "a sick man, too," whose main problem is that he is "forever going around in a delirium of adoration—forever butting in where [he doesn't] belong, looking for something to admire" (5.54-57). Rel-ling wants Gregers to realize that because he is "blind" to his own motivations, he cannot possibly help Hjalmar and in fact is making everything much worse for the Ekdal family.

You'll notice that the student begins by identifying the text in question and then proceeds to state her claim (that the play connects the character "Gre-gers's inability to understand what is really happening within himself to blindness and physical sickness"). She demonstrates her familiarity with the text by summarizing concisely and quoting intelligently; as an audience, we have the sense that the author is guiding the analysis and not simply drop-ping in quotes to fill space. Finally, she works outward from claim, not merely proving that Gregers is physically ill but suggesting that Ibsen, the play's author, is using Gregers's physical illness to symbolize his "blind[ness]" to his internal inadequacies. This analysis is effective, then, because it is concise, demonstrates the author's familiarity with the text, and uses the evidence from the text to advance her thoughts and perceptions.

For additional resources on analysis, please see *Pearson Writer*. In the *Writer's Guide* tab, search for "Analysis Essays."

SAMPLE STUDENT ANALYSIS ESSAY

Jacob Dumbauld

Professor Lahey

UCWR 110

6 February 2015

How to Tame Institutionalized Prejudice

While the human race has come a long way from enslaving each other and slaughtering their own for causes of race and religion, institutionalized racism and oppression are far from gone. Battles are fought every day for the right to free press, freedom of religion, and equal rights among minorities and women. While the prejudices might not be as pronounced as they were just a couple of decades ago, they are still a very real problem. In the battleground of gender and cultural oppression, intelligent and educated authors like Gloria Anzaldúa have pushed for changes through their writing. In her essay "How to Tame a Wild Tongue," Anzaldúa particularly showcases her native Chicano tongue not only to emphasize an inclination towards her cultural roots, but also to provide the non-Spanish-speaking reader a glimpse into the difficult and traumatic experience of not being accepted.

Anzaldúa makes use of powerful anecdotal evidence to help prove this point at the beginning of her essay. She was caught speaking Spanish at recess and her "Anglo" (her word for white American) teacher said, "If you want to be American, speak 'American.' If you don't like it, go back to Mexico where you belong" (34). This kind of blatant racism would be grounds to fire a teacher in the modern day, and Anzaldúa capitalizes on this to deliver her point with maximum effect. Americans, particularly white Americans, born and raised in the United States, will most likely never experience this degree of prejudice and disrespect towards their roots. In addition to all of this, Anzaldúa was just a little girl being told this by a woman three or more times her age. One can only imagine how she felt after being scolded by her teacher, and Anzaldúa fully intends to provoke this kind of thought.

Not long before the rise of 1970s women's rights movements, a young Anzaldúa was told, *"En Boca cerrada no entran moscas.* 'Flies don't enter a closed mouth'" (34). Whether it was from her parents, teachers, or other adults in her life, Anzaldúa makes an important point here. In the time period of Anzaldúa's childhood, it was still common for women to be taught to be polite, and never to voice their own ideas. Commonly held belief stated that women played the role of homemaker, and that the man functioned as the breadwinner. In this kind of role, Anzaldúa was doubly suppressed: firstly on account of her gender and secondly on account of her culture. She was not allowed to speak her mind, especially not in her native tongue. But in quoting this snippet of a point in her life where she could not speak freely, she fights back against the oppressive nature of this advice. In writing her essay, Anzaldúa not only speaks her mind, but also does so in the language that she sees fit.

However, that is not to say that Anzaldúa never struggled emotionally with the oppression and alienation that came with being of a different culture. She voices her pains when she says, "I have so internalized the borderland conflict that sometimes I feel like one cancels out the other and we are zero, nothing, no one. *A veces no soy nada ni nadie. Per hasta cuando no lo soy, lo soy"* (43). Roughly translated, she initially says that at times she feels like nothing to nobody. But Anzaldúa's second claim in Spanish shows her resolve to keep fighting oppression. She says that "even when I wasn't, I was." Her sense of belonging to something greater because of her cultural roots – even when she felt like nothing and nobody – should strike the reader. However, a reader unable to understand Spanish would completely miss out on the power of this quote (which is an exceedingly important part of her reasoning behind putting it in Spanish). This sense of togetherness belongs to her and to those of the same cultural and linguistic background, and that is not something she is willing to give up. She hides that connection in plain view behind the barrier of a different language in order to recreate the effect of isolation and neglect she experienced because of linguistic difference.

Anzaldúa keeps this barrier alive by peppering the rest of her work with Spanish words and phrases. She does this enough that her overall message will not be lost in translation, but those who cannot speak Spanish will be at the very least frustrated. For her, alternating languages serves as a tool to show the reader what it was like to grow up in a world where people did not accommodate her native tongue. She even goes on to say that as long as she feels like she has to accommodate the English speakers, her tongue will be illegitimate (39). These are simply not things that the average American has to deal with on a day-to-day basis. Anzaldúa knows this and takes full advantage of it. She makes any Anglo reader feel guilty by association about the way she has been treated, dispersing the blame for cultural oppression amid a large group.

A final point Anzaldúa makes is the sense of togetherness she feels with those who share her struggles. She uses the example of her experiences watching movies about Mexican culture to further the sense of exclusive community that Chicanos share. She sets the scene by saying, "'*Vámanos a las vistas,*' my mother would call out and we'd all – grandmother, brothers, sister and cousins – squeeze into the car" (Anzaldúa 40). In this example, she gives the trip to the movies a strong sense of belonging by describing a situation where her whole family, her whole community, is crammed together in a single car. Yet, to the reader who can't speak Spanish, they don't understand her mother's request, and hence the reason behind her family's closeness is lost in translation. It instills a sense of exclusion from that community for those who can't speak the language, and Anzaldúa intentionally does this. It is not that she is being selfish, but rather she is trying to recreate the feeling of living in a world where all of the movies celebrated American culture and ignored her own.

In the war against racial stereotypes and oppression, Anzaldúa bombards her oppressors with stories of her frustration and suffering. Anzaldúa's struggle is apparent throughout her essay, but it is seen most powerfully through her use of Chicano Spanish. Nevertheless, through all of the pain came something beautiful: a Chicano culture of which she could be proud. With suffering came a strong sense of community that bore her through her most difficult times. While the reader should feel her frustration and pain through the words on the page, it is just as important that they see what good has come of it. Anzaldúa does not want to make the same mistakes as those who berated her endlessly for being herself. Rather, she wants to give them a glimpse of the pain they've caused, in order to give future Chicanos a fighting chance in a world slowly becoming more accepting of differences.

Works Cited

Anzaldúa, Gloria. "How to Tame a Wild Tongue." *50 Essays: A Portable Anthology*. Ed. Samuel Cohen. Fourth ed. Boston: Bedford/St. Martin, 2007. 33-45. Print.

SYNTHESIS The term "synthesis" has a number of specific meanings, depending on the disciplinary context of the term. In chemistry, synthesis is the process of combining two or more simple substances to make a more complex one. In psychology, synthesis is the integration of attitudes, traits, and responses into a personality. In philosophy, synthesis reconciles two propositions, the thesis and the antithesis, into a new configuration of meaning. In college writing, synthesis involves combining and integrating ideas from two or more sources to develop a new idea. Synthesis writing is sometimes called *discourse synthesis* or *dialectical thinking*, because the task is to put source texts into dialogue, or conversation, with one another (McGinley 227). In a synthesis paper, the writer discusses how two or more texts can be viewed in the light of an organizing theme, structure, or idea and integrates these perspectives to form a complex conclusion or develop a starting point for further inquiry. Synthesis is one of the most effective operations of learning because it requires a constructive thought process. Through synthesis, new ideas are generated; not only our thoughts but also our thought processes are transformed (McGinley 234).

As a university student, you will be required to synthesize in a variety of assignments. For example, in a paper prompt or an exam question, your instructor might ask you to consider the position of theorist C in relation to the views of theorists A and B. In a research paper, you might discuss several arguments about possible causes of the 2008 financial meltdown and use the evidence and viewpoints in these papers to come to your own conclusions about the cause. You might be asked to consider how two authors from the same literary period exemplify the characteristics of that period and how their works have influenced each other. You could be expected to consolidate and explain data from several experiment results. Here are some prompts that ask for a synthesis response:

- Discuss Martin Luther King's notion of an "unjust law" in the light of the Dalai Lama's criteria for "great compassion."

- Compare and contrast what Helen Keller, Malcolm X, and Richard Rodriguez have to say about education and identity.

- How do Robert Reich, Gregory Mantsios, and Fatema Mernissi affect your thinking about class and choice?

Successful synthesis requires mastery of two other writing/thinking processes that we have already described in this chapter: **summary** and **analysis**. First, the writer must be able to demonstrate an understanding of the source texts by objectively restating those ideas in her own words (summary). The writer must also demonstrate an understanding of the component parts of the source text arguments and how these components work together as a whole (analysis). Synthesis completes the process of transformation begun by summary (transforming another's ideas into one's own words) and analysis (selecting, organizing, and interpreting the components of another's ideas) by connecting and integrating the ideas of several texts under a common structure to create a new set of ideas. If the synthesis writer does not have a clear sense of the source texts' meaning, structure, and context, she will have difficulty relating those texts to each other or to her own ideas and experience. The synthesis will fail, and no complex understanding will emerge, if the writer lacks the ability to think *about* and to think *with* source texts.

THE PROCESS OF SYNTHESIS

We might consider the process of synthesis as a journey, a thought excursion on which we lead our readers. Think of Dorothy and her journey through the Land of Oz. She begins with a question that is of interest to her (How can I get home?) and a hypothesis (The Wizard can get me home.). Her experiences in Kansas give her a certain perspective about how to address her problem. Along the way to the Emerald City, Dorothy encounters a variety of characters, each with a different perspective. She learns the story of the Scarecrow and alters the goal of her journey to include his point of view. Together, they meet the Tin Man and connect his knowledge, experience, and goals to their own. The Cowardly Lion's take adds a new dimension. The integration of these perspectives alters the hypothesis about the Wizard's capabilities as the journey moves forward. Just as every argument meets with opposition, Dorothy and company must deal with the counter-objectives of the Wicked Witch of the West as well as those of the Wizard. The travelers take unexpected detours. Each character has a talent or skill that responds to these challenges, just as each text in a synthesis can provide elements of a counterargument or different strategies for pursuing a question. Dorothy's journey culminates in a new thought configuration, one quite different from the original hypothesis (There's no place like home – I was home all along).

Synthesis writing is a complex process, and research and experience tell us that students struggle with this kind of writing. While synthesis may seem to be the result of a linear procedure (reading → summarizing → analyzing → synthesis), such an understanding of synthesizing would be misleading. Research has shown that writers who think of synthesis as the last step in a linear process tend to produce papers that are strung-together summaries and analyses rather than true integrations and connections of ideas (Mateos and Solé 448; McGinley 235).

In order to put texts into conversation with each other, the synthesis writer plays several roles. First, she is a careful reader of texts, placing herself in the position of each text's ideas in order to fully comprehend them. Next, she is a careful summarizer and analyzer, selecting significant ideas from the texts, integrating and connecting them in accordance with an overarching idea that begins as a hypothesis and emerges as a thesis from interaction with the texts. This second role requires note-taking and draft writing, as well as revisiting the texts in order to develop and support a thesis. Then she must become the reader of her own draft, ensuring that she leads the reader clearly through the thought processes that connect the texts she is synthesizing. Successful synthesis writers engage in a recursive process, moving back and forth between reading and writing. Likewise, the structure of the synthesis reflects this recursive process, considering each text in light of both the controlling idea (thesis) and the texts that have already been discussed so far.

STRATEGIES FOR SYNTHESIS WRITING

When you write a synthesis, much of your thought journeying will take place before you begin to write the paper that will be the final product – in reading, note-taking, pre-writing, drafting, and especially *thinking* about the texts you are synthesizing. Careful reading (or viewing, if it is a visual text) and annotation of each source text is a good way to begin. You may find it useful to write a brief summary of each text to consolidate the main and subordinate points of the argument or information firmly in your mind. In note-taking or free-writing, analyze elements of each text such as context, structure, strategy, and tone. As you progress through your note-taking and annotations, you will already be comparing sources in your mind, revisiting the first text in the light of subsequent texts.

A synthesis paper can begin with a question to be explored through multiple source texts. An instructor may ask you to generate your own *issue question* about the texts, or you may be asked to respond to a prompt question. Working with source texts through summary and analysis will lead to the refinement of a controlling idea: the thesis. The synthesis writer will bring the texts into dialogue with each other by asking questions: What do these texts have in common? In what ways do they disagree? Do they differ in the presentation or interpretation of evidence? Do they disagree about underlying beliefs or important assumptions? How do I, as the writer, respond to these texts and the subject or issue under discussion? How do the texts bring my own knowledge and assumptions into question? What insights come out of this interaction among source texts and my own ideas? After considering such questions, you should be able to formulate a tentative thesis or at least an issue question (Ramage, Bean, and Johnson 44-45).

This writer, student Lisa Regganie, begins an exploratory argument by introducing an issue question that she will use as a controlling idea in the synthesis of three texts:

> Growing up in a small farming town, I have witnessed many of the townspeople not continue on to college after high school. They instead go into trades and work blue collar jobs. I am the daughter of parents who did not go to college. My father just did not want to go; he wanted to be a blue collar worker. My mother, on the other hand wanted to go, but her parents could not afford it. My father does not regret not going to college, but my mother regrets it every day that she steps into her dead end job. Both of my parents did not even question sending me to college, and I knew that going to college would be the only way out of the tentative lifestyle I grew up in. Luckily my parents knew this from the day I was born, so they started a college fund early and told

me I could go wherever I wanted to go, be whatever I want to be, and they would bask in the glow of my success. My background leads me to the question: *Does education really open up a whole new world to students?* I explored this idea in three essays by Helen Keller, Richard Rodriguez, and Malcolm X.

The author develops her argument by exploring the three essays with the aim of answering her question. She arrives at her conclusion by considering how each text relates to her issue question:

Helen Keller, Richard Rodriguez, and Malcolm X experience the awakening of different kinds of opportunity through very different modes of education. *In all three cases, opportunity lies within the learner; the opportunity of education is not something I passively receive, but is mine to take, as these students did.* The new outlook on the world I will gain after college will be worth the hard classes, homework, and stress.

In the example above, the author began with a question and answered it in her conclusion. In the following introduction, writer Gabrielle Caputo answers a prompt question (What do Robert Reich and Colin Beavan say about the relationship between happiness and material success, and how do these authors affect your view of this relationship?) in a thesis that synthesizes the views of two authors and her own view:

People are distracted from what is truly important in life because they fixate on making decisions concerning insignificant things and believing that possessions will bring happiness. Robert B. Reich in his article "The Choice Fetish: Blessings and Curses of a Market Idol," and Colin Bevan in his book *No Impact Man* insist upon this, and while they are right, each fails to address how the lack of popular examples of people who are successful without money makes us think having money and items is the sole way to achieve success.

METHODS OF ORGANIZATION

There are two common methods for organizing a synthesis: around the source texts (*block method*) or around the points of connection (*alternating method*).

1. Block Method:

- **Introduction** with claim or issue question.

- Text 1
  - Introduce this source with a brief summary of its ideas, providing its rhetorical context. (Some relevant points for context might include the following: Who is the author(s)? Why should the reader pay attention to what the author(s) has to say about this subject? What is the source's place in the conversation about the claim or issue?) Apply the methods and conventions of good **summary** writing.
  - **Analyze** this source's ideas in relation to the points of connection you have discovered among the source texts and the controlling idea that has emerged from these connections. Respond with your own ideas about the source's position on these points. For example, if your main idea is that knowledge of language opens the door to human relationship and you are discussing Helen Keller's "Everything Has a Name," you will consider how her account of acquiring language demonstrates a new connection to the people in her life.

- Text 2
  - Introduce this source as well, by giving a summary of its main ideas and putting it in context. The difference between this introduction and the first one is that you will transition from the first text to this one by pointing out some similarity or dissimilarity (or both) between the first source text and this one. This connection you establish between texts is crucial and should be discussed in clear, specific fashion. Don't expect your reader to see or make the connection herself. For example, let's say you are introducing Richard Rodriguez's "Private and Public Language" into a conversation about language and human relationship. You might open the sum-

mary by pointing out that while Keller's account tells of how language leads to a discovery of relationships in her immediate family circle, Rodriguez's knowledge of language opens the possibility of public relationships.
- Analyze this source's ideas in relation to the controlling idea, but do so by putting this source in conversation with the previous text as well as your own ideas. How is Rodriguez's experience similar to Keller's, and how is it different?

- Text 3
  - Repeat this process with the third text and with any subsequent texts you discuss. Avoid isolating the texts into a string of separate summaries/analyses. Keep the texts in conversation with each other by discussing points of connection.

- **Conclude** by telling the reader how the conversation among these texts has changed our understanding of the subject under discussion.

2. Alternating Method:

- **Introduction** with claim or issue question. Let's say that in your essay you want to discuss three components of happiness: choice, wealth, and community. You will be considering these ideas in the light of essays by Robert Reich ("The Choice Fetish,") and Gregory Mantsios ("Class in America – 2006") and Colin Beavan's book *No Impact Man*.

- **First point of connection** among the source texts. Describe one of the ideas that these texts have in common. The texts may agree or disagree or take differently nuanced positions on this point.
  - Introduce Text 1 by briefly placing it in its rhetorical context (see questions relevant to rhetorical context in "Text 1" above). Discuss this text's position on this point of connection. For example, Robert Reich sees the overabundance of trivial choices as a nuisance that distracts us from issues that are more important to our ultimate happiness.

- Add Text 2 to the conversation, also briefly placing it in context. Colin Beavan would agree with Reich, in that he believes that most of the choices we make concerning material objects are unnecessary and even destructive.
- Add Text 3 and any subsequent texts in the same way. Include your own ideas in the conversation. Gregory Mantsios would point out that many Americans are too poor to have *enough* choice and would appreciate having some of the choices that Reich and Beavan are complaining about.

- **Second point of connection.** Repeat the process described above, putting the texts in conversation about this point. In the discussion of this and subsequent points, you obviously will not need to introduce the texts and put them in context.

- Continue discussion with connecting point 3.

- **Conclude** by telling the reader how the conversation among these texts has changed our understanding of the subject under discussion.

You can combine these methods by beginning with the block method and then putting sources in conversation with each other using the alternating method. Notice that decisions about the order in which you discuss texts or connecting points will be very important to your argument. You may decide, during the drafting process, to change the order of these elements to enhance the effectiveness of your argument.

Dorothy and friends follow the yellow brick road and signs along the way of the journey. In synthesis writing, you must use *transitional language* to guide readers on the thought journey, helping readers identify the various "speakers" in the conversation and their positions. Use words and phrases to introduce a new perspective and to signal a shift in thought. To introduce the ideas of one text, use active verbs. Don't merely tell us that an author or work "says" something. Try:

- Jones *demonstrates, argues, asserts,* or *reminds . . .*

- This film *portrays, represents,* or *tells the story of . . .*

Use transitions to signal the relations of source ideas to each other:

- While Jones believes _____, Smith takes the opposite view.

- Jones and Smith hold similar positions in all but _____. (Graff, Birkenstein, and Durst 71-75)

Note in the following paragraphs how student writer Judith Howard uses transitional language to put the ideas of her sources in a conversation about the individual and community responsibility:

> **Both Beavan and the Dalai Lama** see individual action as having a powerful impact on more than just the individual. At various places in *No Impact Man,* **Beavan expresses** the idea that individual actions are what constitute collective action. He values the influence of small, individual actions as being critical to the formation of larger movements. **The Dalai Lama speaks** about the impact of one person's actions on another person. He calls for compassion in action, arguing that if our actions lack compassion, they can become dangerous. He makes the point that if we are not considerate of how our individual actions affect the welfare of other people, "inevitably we end up hurting them" (261). **Beavan makes a similar point** concerning the environment: that if we are careless about our impact on the environment, we will cause great harm to it and all other people as a result.
>
> When discussing the individual, **Reich maintains** a position that supports the value of individual choice for the individual's sake **while the Dalai Lama, in contrast,** considers individuals almost entirely as part of a collective. **Reich, despite supporting community,** puts more emphasis on personal desires. After dismissing the smaller, less significant choices that people are able to

make, he calls for us to make the more relevant choices, "Such as what we stand for, to what and whom we're going to commit our lives, and what we want by way of a community and a society" (Reich 66). The focus in this sentence is on the important aspects of life from an individual's perspective. **When the Dalai Lama focuses** on the desires of people, he uses the same phrase various times to describe the most basic desire of humanity: "to be happy and not to suffer" (258). He uses this shared wish to connect all of mankind and to therefore emphasize the responsibility that we have toward each and every other human being.

Remember that the conventions of acknowledging sources apply in this kind of writing. Cite sources in text whenever you summarize, paraphrase, or quote another author's ideas. Provide a Works Cited page that fully and accurately cites all your sources.

For additional resources on synthesis, please see *Pearson Writer*. In the *Writer's Guide* tab, search for "Synthesis Essays".

SAMPLE STUDENT SYNTHESIS ESSAYS

Emmylou Ford

Professor Weller

UCWR 110

Synthesis Essay

3 March 2015

From Emmylou to Ami Gaye: A Perspective on Multicultural Identity

"*Ey, Ami Gaye!*" It was a name I often heard while walking down the sandy pathways of my village in rural Senegal, but it took months before I felt like it was my identity. Upon arriving in my new home, I was given a new name and a new way of life. For months, I resisted when told to eat with my hands, attend Muslim prayer, and correct the pronunciation of my distorted Wolof words. I struggled to balance a new culture with my old identity while still wanting to be accepted by this new community despite my blatant differences. Bhatia Mukherjee's essay "Two Ways to Belong in America" and Amy Tan's essay "Mother Tongue" touch on these struggles of multiculturalism. In Mukherjee's essay, she explores the differences between herself and her sister as they navigate immigration and identity. Tan, in her essay, describes the effect her mother has had on her perception of her environment. By means of these relationships, Tan and Mukherjee explore how language and assimilation have impacted their multicultural identity.

Tan's ability to oscillate between Chinese and American culture allows her to observe how language can be a barrier when trying to be accepted in a new culture. Tan's use of anecdotes is powerful in demonstrating the sharp contrast between the treatment that she and her mother receive due to language. Tan builds the reader's vicarious frustration as she progresses from her previously ashamed view of her mother, to the anecdote of the baffled stockbroker, and then to the incident with the lost CAT scan. In the latter anecdote, Tan portrays the staff at the hospital as uncompassionate when Tan's mother states her anxiety over the scan in light of her husband and son's death due to brain tumors; however, the staff "did not seem to have any sympathy" that compelled them to find her results (420). This treatment ceases when a staff member communicates directly to Tan, who speaks "perfect English" (420). This demonstrates the mentality of disregard toward those who speak English with an accent or with incorrect grammar.

Mukherjee's narrative also showcases the barriers immigrants face; however, she addresses the struggles they face when confronted with the choice of assimilation. Mukherjee portrays her sister, Mira's, anger over the law reform that discriminates against resident non-citizens. After years of dedicating her "professional skills into the improvement of [America]," she states that she "feel[s] used...manipulated and discarded" (292). However, by comparing Mira's situation to a similar one Mukherjee faced in Canada, Muhkerjee implies that Mira is responsible for her struggles since she did not decide to simply obtain American citizenship. Muhkerjee chose to be in a place that allowed her to be "a part of the community [she] adopted," arguing that the only way to be accepted and appreciated by society is to assimilate, culturally and legally, to the new country (293). Mira's aversion to assimilation is a choice that distances her from her new country, whereas Tan's mother's struggles in her new country are arbitrated by others.

Despite the barriers immigrants face, Tan's capability to navigate language has allowed her to build connections, especially with her mother. Tan's ability to understand her mother's "broken" or "limited" English is imperative in establishing the dynamic of their relationship (419). The transcription of her mother's dialogue is a powerful tool to showcase the apparent challenges in understanding her speech. Tan's later description of her attachment to her mother and this style of speech, despite its difficulty, produces a sense of respect from the reader. This is further developed when Tan describes the protective ways in which she caters to her mother, mainly through speaking on her mother's behalf. Tan needs to defend her mother since her speech has "helped shape the way [she] saw things, expressed things, [and] made sense of the world" (419).

Like Tan, Mukherjee can also compare herself to familial relationships and come to a better understanding of her multicultural identity. Using Mira as a calibration for assimilation, Mukherjee is able to look at her own sense of belonging with satisfaction. Looking at their immigrant journey, Mukherjee comments that "there could not be a wider divergence" (292). While Mira clings to her "saris [and] delightfully accented English," Mukherjee "surrender[ed] those" for the "trauma of self-transformation" (292, 293). Mukherjee's diction elicits negative and painful connotations, but she also states that she "married" America and "embraced" her immigrant status (292). Willing to undergo the arduous pursuit of citizenship and cultural assimilation, Mukherjee, unlike her sister, also gained acceptance. Unfortunately, unlike Tan's multicultural relationship with her mother, Mukherjee distanced herself from her sister through this assimilation.

Due to my experience abroad, I can empathize with both Mukherjee's and Tan's perspective on multicultural identity. Seeing how language is our primary means of communication and understanding, it's fitting that Tan argues that it drives our perception of the world. I can attest that when I speak Wolof because I very much embody Ami Gaye, a girl who tends to relationships differently than Emmylou Ford. This is partly due to how culture drives the language but is also in response to how others treat me when I speak "broken" Wolof. As much as I tried to straddle the multicultural line, I was never fully accepted, which is imperative to assimilation, as we saw with Tan's mother and both the Mukherjee sisters. Bharati Mukherjee was able to overcome some of her flagrant differences, unlike Tan's mother, and assimilate. The Mukherjee sisters and I understand that assimilation comes at a great cost: giving up parts of oneself. As trivial as it may seem, I was never willing to neglect the comfort of pants and don a wrap-around *pagne*, a traditional garment made from a rectangular strip of fabric fashioned into a loincloth or wrapped on the body to form a short skirt. For this reason I could never be looked at as an accepted equal.

While language and physicality hinder acceptance, as in my own case as well as Tan's mother and the Mukherjee sisters, so does the choice to surrender one's own traditions and identity, a decision Mira and I struggled with.

Mukherjee and Tan's relationships help them better understand their personal identity, but also their identity within the cultures they navigate. Tan's unique communication with her mother is a form of intimacy that defines her perception of self, which attributes to her interpretation of the world. Tan is able to transcend both American and Chinese culture, while Mukherjee stakes her identity firmly in American culture. By comparing herself to her sister, these choices are affirmed. The struggles of immigrants, second-generation children, and even travelers spawn from how we interact with the world. My name, whether it's Ami Gaye, Emily, or Emmylou, is how I identify myself but also how the world recognizes me. This is why relationships are so central to identity, as with Tan and Mukherjee; it is an understanding of self that is affirmed by those around us.

Works Cited

Mukherjee, Bharati. "Two Ways to Belong in America." *50 Essays: A Portable Anthology*. Ed. Samuel Cohen. 4th ed. Boston: Bedford/St. Martin's, 2007.290293. Print.

Tan, Amy. "Mother Tongue." *50 Essays: A Portable Anthology*. Ed. Samuel Cohen. 4th ed. Boston: Bedford/St. Martin's, 2004. 417-423. Print.

RESEARCHED ARGUMENT

A Research-Based Argument vs. An Informational Research Project

In UCWR 110, you will be required to compose a research paper that makes an argument. This requirement may be different from research projects that you have done in the past.

In high school, students are often asked to do research projects for the purpose of gathering information and presenting that information to the reader. This type of project is akin to creating an encyclopedia entry or Wikipedia page.

However, the purpose of the research assignment is different in UCWR 110. Most often, the main purpose is to develop an argument based on the research you have done. While the project will of course require you to do substantial information gathering, in your paper you will be expected to develop an argument and shape the paper around a thesis. Students sometimes struggle with this argumentative aspect of the assignment because they see research as strictly collecting information about a topic. As you conduct your research, you should therefore not only gather information but also identify the different debates your sources are engaged in. These debates can point you toward a more specific issue around which you can structure your argument.

Here is an illustration of the difference between an informational project and a research-based argument: Suppose you are interested in the protest movement against the Vietnam War in the 1960s and 1970s. For an informational project you would gather material about the leading anti-war figures and the major anti-war organizations, their reasons for opposing the war, and the methods of protest they employed. Indeed, your paper itself might be organized around these sub-topics. However, for a research-based argument, you would gather the same information but would also investigate the various debates among historians about the antiwar movement. There are a number of these, but one prominent debate focuses on the effectiveness of the movement in helping bring the war to an end.

As a researcher, you could enter this conversation about the movement by researching and analyzing the different interpretations of its effectiveness. In your paper, you would frame the debate in your introduction, present your broad stance on the issue of the movement's effectiveness, and then structure your paper around the reasons that support your argument. Be sure to make your argument throughout the paper. Each paragraph should advance your argument in some way. Beware of the misguided perception that a research-based argument is just an informational paper with your personal opinion tacked on in the introduction and conclusion.

Writing as Inquiry or Exploratory Research
While some instructors may require a researched argument, others require a paper in which you conduct research as a means to explore or inquire into an issue you find compelling. As discussed above, in order to produce a research-based argument, you need to gather information, identify key questions related to your issue, and consider different views on the subject. Then you structure your paper around a thesis on the issue. But in an exploratory essay the focus and content of your paper will be the very type of research and thinking you do *before* writing a thesis-driven research paper. Rather than making an argument about a specific issue and developing that argument throughout your paper as you would in a researched-based argument, an exploratory essay offers a sort of analytical overview of your process of discovery.

Although it does not present an overarching argument, an exploratory essay does nevertheless involve a great deal of **analysis**, **synthesis**, and evaluation of the sources and their views on the topic. This is the major distinction between an exploratory essay and an informational one. Informational essays tend to focus primarily on summary and contain only minimal analysis, synthesis, and evaluation. An exploratory essay on the antiwar movement of the 1960s, for example, would not only summarize the information you have gathered but would also lay out the main debates or differences in interpretation that historians have offered on the issue. In addition, and perhaps most importantly, it would offer some analysis of the strengths and weaknesses of different views and point the reader toward the more convincing ones, even though it might not necessarily come to definitive conclusions about the debates it has reviewed.

PLANNING AND TIME-MANAGEMENT

One of the greatest challenges of writing a successful research paper involves planning the various stages of your project and setting aside sufficient time for each. One reason a research paper can seem so daunting is that we tend to see it as one huge task. This can make us feel overwhelmed and lead to a deadly pattern of procrastination. However, effective planning and time-management can reduce the stress of a big project and help you produce a more successful research paper.

Your instructor will likely break down parts of the project into various stages. Typically, an instructor may require you to submit a proposal, do an annotated bibliography, write a draft for peer review, and revise that draft for submission. However, you should break those tasks down as well. Instead of seeing the project as a series of deadlines and assignments (a sort of "teacher-centered" or "assignment-centered" view), approach it from a writer's point of view. This means trying to see it as a set of discrete yet related tasks that can be tackled at various stages and even re-visited as you proceed.

As a writer, in order to meet the deadlines and do the assignments, you are faced with the following: choosing a topic, finding sources, making notes, drafting a thesis, planning and organizing your paper, writing a draft, revising, and editing. This is quite a bit, but by tackling the various tasks in stages and seeing how they relate to one another, you can keep the project manageable.

Here are some suggestions for planning and time-management:

- Start exploring topics soon after you've received the assignment. You will likely have to narrow, refine, and even discard topics before you settle on one. This takes time, so don't put it off.

- Set aside ample time to find sources. Plan for multiple research sessions, and consider asking for help from your instructor or a research librarian.

- Avoid doing your research in one big push before a deadline. You should regularly re-examine the sources you have in order to consider what kinds of sources you still need to find.

- Adopt an effective and organized note-taking system. There's nothing worse than scrambling to find that great quotation you want to plug in but have lost track of.

- Develop a tentative thesis early on. Your argument will likely change, but having a thesis will help you focus and manage your research more efficiently.

- Create an outline before drafting, ideally one organized around your argument, i.e., its thesis, the reasons supporting that thesis, and/or the major counter-arguments you will be addressing. Elaborating on your argument is crucial to your success, so structuring your outline around its key components, rather than broad topics or sources, will streamline the drafting process and help you produce a draft that is focused and convincing.

- Set aside extensive time for drafting. Unlike other assignments, with a research paper you are juggling large amounts of material. Even with a strong outline, synthesizing this material on the page can be challenging and time-consuming.

- Draft in stages. Consider beginning with a section you feel comfortable with. We often assume that drafting is a linear process. It rarely is. Starting with the parts you find easier to write can build confidence and momentum for those more challenging aspects of the project.

- Revise in stages as well. Just like with research and drafting, trying to revise in one big push is generally ineffective. Identify two to four priorities for revision, begin with one or two of those, proceed methodically, and then move on to new priorities in later revision sessions.

- Edit for continuity and coherence as well as grammar and style. Because this is a longer paper that you will have drafted and revised in stages, it will often need continuity editing that ensures that the various parts are unified and connected. Make sure you have developed your main argument and asserted your voice in each section.

The Recursive Nature of the Research Process
The suggestions above might make the writing of the research paper seem like a straightforward, step-by-step procedure; however, writing an effective research paper, like almost all writing, is a more recursive than linear process. Keep in mind that many of these seemingly discrete tasks are overlapping. When executing a new stage of the process, you may need to return to previous tasks.

Take, for example, doing research and finding sources. Chances are that once you've chosen a topic, your instructor will require you to submit an annotated bibliography in which you document and summarize your sources, often a specific number of them. At this stage, it can feel like the research process is complete, and if you are lucky, it may be. However, producing the annotated bibliography often highlights gaps in your research or points to further questions that need to be addressed before you start drafting. This will require more research. Even as you are drafting or after peer review, you may continue to identify gaps in your knowledge. As a result, you will have to do additional research to shore up your paper.

For additional information and ideas, see *Pearson Writer*. In the *Writer's Guide* tab, search for "'How do you develop a research project?'", "'How do you schedule a research project?'", and "'How do you organize a writing project?'". Also, under the *Writer's Guide* tab, under the 'Browse Content' heading, click on "Research" for a broader listing of resources for the researched argument essay assignment.

CHOOSING AND NARROWING A TOPIC
The process of choosing a topic is another highly challenging part of the research process. While occasionally a writer quickly comes up with a viable, engaging focus, the process of choosing a topic and narrowing its focus can be complex, time-consuming, and – let's admit it – frustrating. Yet producing a successful paper depends greatly on choosing a topic that is clearly defined

and engaging. Moreover, having a well-defined topic can make the subsequent stages of the process more focused and efficient.

Here are some guidelines for choosing and narrowing your topic:

- To get started, use whatever idea-generating techniques you find valuable. These can include brainstorming, free-writing, talking to others, or perusing newspapers and magazines.

- Find a topic that truly interests you. Working on something that you are genuinely curious about will make the process far more engaging and rewarding.

- Beware of stale, hand-me-down topics like abortion or capital punishment. While these can be approached in interesting ways, they are overdone and broad, and students often choose them simply because they seem familiar and easy rather than genuinely interesting.

- Revise your topic as you proceed. As you research and acquire knowledge of your subject, your interest and focus will likely shift and narrow. Follow your interests.

- Consider focusing on a sub-topic within your larger topic. This is related to the suggestion above. Often in the process of researching, planning, and even drafting, we discover our topic is too broad. Rather than finding an entirely new topic, the more effective strategy is to focus on a sub-topic, i.e., a topic within your original topic. While students are often reluctant to narrow in this way because they feel they may not have enough to say, the truth is that focusing on a sub-topic often allows the writer to develop a more interesting and complex argument.

- Use sources to identify specific issues or questions. Your topic should be a debatable one, so your sources will, in one form or another, be framing the debatable issues within that topic. You as a writer are entering the conversation these sources are engaged in, so look for the questions and issues the sources are addressing, and feel free to focus on a specific issue that they have identified.

As the above suggestions indicate, finalizing a topic usually involves research, often substantial amounts of it. While it is useful to brainstorm and reflect on your interests in order to generate possible topics, you will likely need to do some preliminary research before you can settle comfortably into a topic. Later in the process, as your research becomes more thorough and your knowledge of the subject increases, you may have to refine your topic to reflect your greater understanding.

The process of refining your topic can continue right up to the submission of your final draft. As you draft, go through peer review, and revise your paper, you may realize that you want to focus more on one specific aspect of the topic and will need to re-work your paper accordingly.

A Topic vs. An Issue
While we have thus far spoken primarily of choosing a topic, the term "topic" can be misleading because it is so general. Since you are developing an argument, it might be more helpful to think of addressing an issue or, perhaps even better, answering a question. Looking at the process as choosing a topic can lead us to rather broad and ultimately unmanageable topics. But if we think about addressing an issue or answering a question, we can give our work focus and ensure that we are producing an argumentative essay.

But what's the difference between a topic and an issue? A topic is typically rather general and doesn't necessarily point to a debate, while an issue points to a debate or a debatable question. Here's an example that illustrates the distinction between a topic and an issue and also delineates the process of moving from a topic to a specific issue and question:

Suppose after reading essays by Malcolm X and Carolyn Bird you decide you are interested in the topic of college education. However, writing about "college education" is obviously too broad, so you have to narrow your focus. What has intrigued you perhaps is the suggestion that college education is not necessary or valuable for most people. Now you are moving toward an issue.

This is still somewhat broad, however. Now you might consider why you have asked yourself this question. You realize that you have been challenged by Malcolm X's claim that college life, with its parties and panty raids, is actually a distraction from genuine learning. In addition, Malcolm X demonstrates that he has educated himself better than any college could have, while Bird claims that, because we have such wide access to materials now, pretty much anyone can educate himself or herself in the way colleges promise to. You are torn because you recognize some truth in Malcolm X's and Bird's arguments but also value your own college experience. You know that so much of college life is distracting yet so much is rewarding as well. Now you are refining the issue even further. You might arrive at the following question: "Given the problems and value present in college life, how can colleges create an environment that better fosters the kind of education Malcolm achieved on his own?" This question would point you toward research on the goals of college education, the main problems in student achievement, and the ways these problems have been addressed.

Pragmatic Issues vs. Conceptual Issues
Determining whether you want to approach your topic from a pragmatic or a conceptual angle can help you narrow your focus.

Almost every paper will address both pragmatic and conceptual issues, but most successful ones tend to focus primarily on one or the other. The difference between the two is this: a pragmatic focus will ask readers to do something or adopt a specific action to solve a problem while a conceptual focus will ask readers to gain understanding or adopt a belief regarding an issue or problem.

Conceptual and pragmatic problems of course overlap; you can't solve a problem without some conceptual understanding of the issue, and conceptual thinking can point you to pragmatic solutions. However, it is best to identify whether your main purpose is to create understanding (conceptual) or if it is to urge a solution or action (pragmatic) (Williams and Colomb 70).

Let's return to the topic of college education mentioned earlier in this section. Suppose that in addition to having read Malcolm X and Carolyn Bird on education, you have read articles about the failure of universities to adequately prepare students for the world of work. You've found general agreement about this. If you were to adopt a *conceptual* approach to the topic, you might research the reasons for this failure: Why are college graduates consistently under-prepared for professional careers? This might involve debates over issues of curriculum, standards, student attitudes, or employer needs.

You would focus your research on finding material that addresses these conceptual issues. In your conclusion, you might briefly address the implications of your conceptual analysis for pragmatic solutions, but this would not be the main focus on the paper.

However, you could also tackle this topic from a *pragmatic* angle by examining solutions to the problem: How can colleges better prepare students for careers and the world of work? While this approach would have to address some conceptual issues about the causes of the problem, your main focus – and the overwhelming proportion of your paper – would analyze possible solutions in order to propose the best course of action. What are colleges doing to better prepare students? What seems to be working or not working? Based on your research, what would you recommend as an effective approach or set of approaches to solving this problem?

For further information and ideas, see *Pearson Writer*. In the *Writer's Guide*, search for "'How do you find a research topic?'", "'How to refine your topic'", and "'How to write research papers'".

SAMPLE STUDENT RESEARCHED ARGUMENT

Ross Carpino

Professor Quirk

UCWR 110

05 Dec 2014

Plan B: The Only Plan

After many years of age restrictions, the emergency contraceptive Plan B One-Step was recently made available to women universally. Many find that this change in policy regarding the emergency contraceptive pill will increase promiscuity among teenagers. Others feel that there was not substantial medical and scientific evidence to implement an age restriction in the first place. Ultimately, the debate boils down to whether or not adolescent females are capable of understanding the pill's use and being able to use such a medication correctly. However, females who are old enough to ovulate are old enough to make the decision to use Plan B One-Step responsibly. Therefore, Plan B One-Step should be available to females of all ages without a prescription or an age requirement. What is at stake here is providing females the right to choose whether having a child is right for them or not, regardless of age.

A recent court ruling from Judge Edward R. Korman, an appointed United States District Judge for the Eastern District of New York, ordered that the most common emergency contraceptive medication, Plan B One-Step, be made available over the counter without any age restrictions (Belluck). The judge's main argument for his ruling was politics. By accusing the Obama administration of "putting politics ahead of science" Korman deduced that the decision to only sell Plan B One-Step behind the counter to females over the age of 17 was not made based on scientific evidence (Belluck). Instead the decision was made based on political moves for Obama's reelection. In 2011, prime campaigning time for reelection, the Health and Human Services secretary, Kathleen Sebelius countermanded the F.D.A.'s decision to make Plan B One-Step universally available. Judge Korman comments on this decision, declaring, "the secretary's action was politically motivated … and scientifically unjustified" (Belluck). In 2011, the F.D.A. found no scientific reasoning to prohibit selling Plan B One-Step universally, yet Sebelius saw an opportunity to make a political move to help Obama's reelection. If the Food and Drug Administration saw no reason in 2011 to prohibit the pill's sale, and no scientific evidence has come to show any chronic medical consequences, then there is no reason that the pill should be regulated.

The Center for Drug Evaluation and Research, or CDER, also did a review for Plan B One-Step's application and found its own scientific solution. As they worked to find its solution, the CDER experimented to determine whether younger females were able to understand the use of Plan B One-Step (Bailey). Based on their results, they found that the emergency contraceptive was "safe and effective for adolescents" and that "adolescent females understood the product was not for routine use … and would not protect them against sexually transmitted diseases" (Bailey). One of the few points in this argument which is supported by the CDER's research is that younger females are capable of understanding what Plan B One-Step is used for as well as what it does not protect against. As the government continues to put politics ahead of science, it is the young women who fail to meet the legislated age requirements who suffer the consequences.

The main opposition to selling Plan B One-Step without any age restrictions is that it causes abortions of developing fetuses. However, this is a complete misconception. Plan B One-Step is not an abortifacient medication, meaning that the medication will not prohibit the growth and development of a fetus, nor will it stop a pregnancy (Stangl). Plan B One-Step is the most commonly sold emergency contraceptive in the United States, which works only hormonally (Stangl). Through the medical lens, the purpose of taking this emergency contraceptive is to inhibit either ovulation or fertilization by making the endometrium an inhospitable environment (Stangl). In the words of Rebecca Stangl, an assistant professor of philosophy at the University of Virginia, "The longstanding consensus in the medical community is that pregnancy begins when a fertilized egg implants itself in the uterus... and everyone agrees that emergency contraction cannot cause the termination of a fertilized egg that has already implanted itself in the uterus" (Stangl).

Therefore, the argument that Plan B One-Step is an abortifacient medication is invalid. Those who oppose the sale of this emergency contraceptive on the grounds that it causes abortions ignore the clear scientific evidence stating that Plan B One-Step cannot be classified as an abortifacient medication. How can a pill such as Plan B One-Step cause abortions if a life was never conceived to begin with? It can't, proving the common misconception that Plan B One-Step is an abortifacient medication invalid.

Even if we overlook the scientific facts which prove that Plan B One-Step is not an abortifacient medication, we can still permit its use using Thomas Aquinas's doctrine of double effect. Within the field of philosophy the doctrine of double effect is often "invoked to explain the permissibility of an action that causes a serious harm … as a side effect of promoting some good end" (McIntyre). If we evaluate the use of Plan B One-Step through a moral lens, the doctrine of double effect enables its use. In the words of Rebecca Stangl, "If one accepts the doctrine of double effect, there are circumstances that still permit its [Plan B One-Step] use" (Stangl). When a female takes Plan B One-Step as an emergency contraceptive, the serious harm would hypothetically come from aborting the life of a developing fetus. Yet the "good end" would be the female does not conceive a child. By using the doctrine of double effect, philosophy has proved that even if Plan B One-Step was an abortifacient drug, which it is not, then its use would still be permitted. By allowing females everywhere to make the choice of what outcome will provide their life with a "good end," we permit the use of the emergency contraceptive.

A second opposition that many agree with is for Plan A, also known as abstinence. *The Washington Times* in their editorial *Shelving Plan B* discusses the benefits of choosing Plan A over Plan B. *The Washington Times* states that "By slowly rolling back the age at which Plan B is available ... Congress can't build the momentum needed to ditch Plan B in favor of Plan A ... which works every time" ("Shelving Plan B"). While their argument that "Plan A works every time" is a valid one, it is unrealistic to expect all adolescents to abstain from engaging in sexual activities. Statistics regarding the sexual activity among American adolescents show that 48% of American adolescents have engaged in sexual intercourse by the age of 17 ("American Teens' Sexual and Reproductive Health"). The previous age restriction for purchasing Plan B One-Step was 17. If we put that into context, 48% of American adolescents have engaged in sexual intercourse by the age of 17, and are theoretically at risk of pregnancy. These adolescents who are younger than the age restriction still need to have access to this emergency contraceptive if they are engaging in sexual intercourse. If Plan A fails, females should not be punished with the possibility of having a child solely because Plan B One-Step has a scientifically unjustified age restriction. Plan A is a good plan; however, when Plan A fails, females of all ages should have Plan B One-Step available to them if they need it.

As Plan B One-Step has continued to have scientifically unjustified age restriction, it is also in violation of the Fourteenth Amendment. Vanessa Lu, a legal extern at the U.S. Securities & Exchange Commission and a research assistant to Professor Neil Williams of Loyola University Chicago School of Law, clarifies that "Under the Due Process Clause of the Fourteenth Amendment, the Supreme Court has stated that each person is entitled to 'a right of personal privacy'" (Lu). She continues on to explain how the constitution never plainly states what a "right of privacy" is, but it does however guarantee an individual "the interest in independence in making certain kinds of important decisions" (Lu). What this means is that the government cannot interfere with important choices which are protected as a "right of privacy." One of these "rights of privacy" is the choice to use contraceptives or to not use contraceptives. The Fourteenth Amendment protects against the government imposing their views on important decisions such as who should be able to use emergency contraceptives. Therefore, without scientific evidence, denying someone access to an emergency contraceptive, such as Plan B One-Step, due to age restrictions is a direct violation of the Fourteenth Amendment. Denying a female under the age of 17 access to Plan B One-Step without a prescription from a physician violates that woman's "right of privacy" and is a direct violation of the Fourteenth Amendment.

A third opposition which opposes the sale of Plan B One-Step without age restrictions is that it will increase promiscuity among minors. This unvalidated argument is commonly viewed as an endeavor by the government to control sexual behavior among minors (Lu). In the words of Vanessa Lu, "The FDA has not presented evidence to show that over-the-counter access to Plan B [One-Step] will increase unprotected sex among minors nor has it shown that minors will use more common reliable forms of contraceptives any less" (Lu). Increased promiscuity among minors is an assumption made by the FDA which ignores "conclusive scientific evidence that proves access to Plan B [One-Step] without a prescription does not increase health-related risks to minors"

(Lu). This is more than just another unjustified argument, as it is also another example of how politics is being put ahead of science on the topic of emergency contraceptives.

Judge Edward R. Korman's decision to order the FDA to revoke its age restriction on Plan B One-Step brought justice to this controversy. The FDA must allow the emergency contraceptive to be sold without age restrictions; otherwise they are limiting a minor's right to access emergency contraceptives and in a direct violation of the Fourteenth Amendment. Until the FDA finds evidence to prove medical side effects for females under the age of 17 or 18 who take Plan B One-Step, they have no reason to limit the sale of the emergency contraceptive. Since Plan B One-Step is not an abortifacient medication, Plan A only works around 50% of the time, and promiscuity will not be increased among minors, the only conceivable conclusion is to permit the sale of the emergency contraceptive without age restrictions. After all, the age restriction is a violation of the Fourteenth Amendment.

Ultimately, the argument over Plan B One-Step comes down to the freedom for females everywhere, regardless of age, to be able to choose what is right for them. Without scientific evidence to demonstrate any reason why Plan B One-Step shouldn't be available universally, there is no reason why people should disapprove of the emergency contraceptive. Also, as it is medically proven that the emergency contraceptive in no way causes abortions, the main counterargument is invalid. Without scientific evidence to support the restrictions that are implemented on the emergency contraceptive, there is no logical reason to have them. Judge Edward R. Korman clearly made the long overdue decision to make Plan B One-Step universally available to females, finally putting science ahead of politics.

Works Cited

"American Teens' Sexual and Reproductive Health." *Guttmacher Institute.* Guttmacher Institute. May 2014. Web. 1 Nov. 2014.

Bailey, Ronald. "Obama, Plan B, Fear of Promiscuity, Sex and the Single Teen." *Hit & Run.* Reason Foundation. 9 Apr. 2013. Web. 2. Nov. 2014.

Belluck, Pam. "Judge Strikes Down Age Limits on Morning-After Pill." *The New York Times* 5 Apr. 2013: A1-A3. *Academic Search Complete.* Web. 3 Nov. 20214.

Lu, Vanessa. "The Plan B Age Restriction Violates a Minor's Right to Access Contraceptives." *Family Law Quarterly* 44.3 (2010): 398-401. *Academic Search Complete.* Web. 31 October 2014.

McIntyre, Alison. "Doctrine of Double Effect." *Stanford Encyclopedia of Philosophy.* Metaphysics Research Lab, 23 Sep. 2014. Web. 3 Nov. 2014.

"Shelving Plan B." Editorial. *The Washington Times.* 3 May 2013. Web. 26 October 2014.

Stangl, Rebecca. "Plan B and the Doctrine of Double Effect." *Hastings Center Report* 39.4 (2009): 21-25. *Academic Search Complete.* Web. 31 October 2014.

LIBRARY SERVICES AT LOYOLA

Writing a research paper can be a daunting task, even for experienced researchers. Fortunately, dedicated help and effective research resources are always available at Loyola libraries. A librarian will be part of your UCWR class this semester, and librarians might participate in other classes you take. Librarians and other library staff are committed to helping students do their best work. For them, no question is too small or silly, so do not hesitate to ask for assistance.

LIBRARY REFERENCE DESK

Librarians assist students on the second floor of the Information Commons on the Lakeshore Campus and in Lewis Library at the Water Tower Campus. You can drop by or schedule an appointment in advance. There is also online help; you can access assistance through a chat connection or by sending questions to librarians as text messages. Details about all of these services are available through the library's website.

LIBRARY CIRCULATION DESK

Library staff at the circulation desk in Cudahy and Lewis Libraries will help you check out books, pick up materials on hold or requested through Interlibrary Loan, and check out course reserve materials.

LIBRARY INFORMATION RESOURCES

A well-written, research-based argument is supported by quality information resources. Locating these resources, especially those from scholarly sources, requires learning about library catalogs and research databases.

Before you are ready to delve into scholarly sources on an unfamiliar topic, you will usually need to consult reference sources, or sources of background information. Many reference sources are available online, but some classic ones still exist only in print. Reference sources may be found using a library catalog or other search aids, but often the best method is simply asking a librarian for a referral. A librarian will suggest at least one reference source to your UCWR class during class with you this semester.

Once you have basic knowledge about a topic, you will be ready to begin searching a library catalog or research database. Our library supports various catalogs which may be accessed through the library's website. These catalogs help locate books, both print and electronic, in the library's collections. A librarian will introduce the catalogs to your class, but you are encouraged to experiment and contact librarians with your questions.

The library also provides students with access to hundreds of databases, most of them tied to research in specific subject areas. In UCWR classes, librarians will focus on one general database that can be used for nearly any topic. Databases are linked from the library's website, both by title and by subject area through our Research Guides (see below).

Your instructor and the research librarian who works with your class will be eager to help you navigate through the college-level research project. Make good use of these individuals and their expertise. But successful research requires perhaps more independent work than any other type of writing assignment. Because of this, Loyola libraries have created a number of useful web pages that can help facilitate the research project. On the library web page (libraries.luc.edu), you can access "Research Guides" that are organized by disciplines such as Anthropology, Environmental Studies, and Physics. Among these, moreover, is a guide designed especially for UCWR. This guide may be your most useful electronic link.

The Research Guide for UCWR (libguides.luc.edu/UCWR?hs=a) contains a number of extremely useful tabs that address various areas of research. Some of these, such as "Types of Academic Sources," provide helpful overviews. Others, such as "Evaluating Sources" and "The Research Question," reinforce information and skill sets you will need to compose a successful research paper. Perhaps most importantly, other tabs provide links to the most used and most useful databases, as well as the catalogs. Consider opening this page and working from there whenever you are conducting your research. Make it your home base for each research session, and you should be able to navigate swiftly among the various tabs and links the library has designed to serve your research needs.

WORKS CITED

Caputo, Gabrielle. "The Lies We Waste Our Lives On." *Communities in Conversation: Environmental Issues and Green Activism.* Eds. Sherrie Weller, et al. Loyola University Chicago, 2011. 50-51. Print.

Fitzgerald, F. Scott.

Felius, Marleen, et al. "On the Breeds of Cattle—Historic and Current Classifications." *Diversity* 3 (2011): 660-692. *Academic Search Premier.* Web. 26 Sept. 2012.

Graff, Gerald, Cathy Birkenstein, and Russel Durst. *They Say/I Say: The Moves That Matter in Academic Writing with Readings.* 2nd ed. New York: W. W. Norton, 2012.

Hidi, Suzanne, and Valerie Anderson. "Producing Written Summaries: Task Demands, Cognitive Operations, and Implications for Instruction." *Review of Educational Research* 56.4 (Winter 1986): 473-493. *JSTOR.* Web. 25 June 2012.

Howard, Judith. "The Need for Connection." *Communities in Conversation: Environmental Issues and Green Activism.* Eds. Sherrie Weller, et al. Loyola University Chicago, 2011. 47-49. Print.

Howard, Rebecca Moore. *Writing Matters.* New York: McGraw-Hill, 2011. Print.

Maclellan, Effie. "Reading to Learn." *Studies in Higher Education* 22.3 (Oct. 1997): 277-289. *Academic Search Premier.* Web. 28 June 2012.

Mateos, Mar, and Isabel Sol. "Synthesising Information from Various Texts: A Study of Procedures and Products at Different Educational Levels." *European Journal of Psychology of Education* 24.1 (2009) 435-451. Print.

McGinley, William. "The Role of Reading and Writing While Composing from Sources." *International Reading Association* 27.3 (1992) 227-248.

Morgan, Teyana. "Summary Assignment." 27 February 2012. MS.

Ramage, John D., John C. Bean, and June Johnson. *Writing Arguments: A Rhetoric with Readings.* Brief 9th Ed. Boston: Pearson, 2011.

Regannie, Lisa. "A Whole New World." 27 Oct. 2012. MS.

Strahan, Linda, Kathleen Moore, and Michael Heumann. *Write It: A Process Approach to College Essays.* Dubuque: Kendall Hunt, 2011. Print.

Williams, Joseph M., and Gregory G. Colomb. *The Craft of Argument.* 2nd ed. New York: Longman, 2003. Print.

Yu, Guoxing. "The Shifting Sands in the Effects of Source Text Summarizability on Summary Writing." *Assessing Writing* 14 (2009): 116-137. *ScienceDirect.* Web. 25 June 2012.